HOW TO
IDENTIFY AND ADDRESS
CRITICAL GLOBAL AND
US PROBLEMS AND SOLVE THEM
IN SIXTY YEARS OR LESS

BY

A Concerned US Senior Citizen

ISBN: 9798364495129

Table of Contents

Introduction

I was born in April 1936. Accordingly, as George Carling would have put it: I recently 'hit' the ripe age of 86; thankfully, in good health and sound mind.

Some might say: "What could I possibly learn from an old geezer!?" On the other hand however, it is said: "Live and Learn", thus, the longer you live, the more you learn, accordingly, it seems that wisdom comes with age. A famous French adage, roughly translated states: "If only the elderly could … if only the young knew"!?

The views that I will express evolved over several decades and are based on my academic and professional experience as an architect and urban planner. Therefore, the text will unfold by citing the particular aspects of my education and professional knowledge which led me to write this book. This prepares the reader for appreciating the text that follows which covers what the title promises to accomplish.

Chapter 1

"Beauty is in the Eye of the Beholder" / Beliefs Leading to Action as Subjective

I graduated as an architect with flying colors. This qualified me to apply for and get a scholarship to pursue a doctorate degree in architecture in a reputable university. I started my assignment in 1959, and it took me a couple of years to meet the university's requirements to qualify for Doctoral research which I successfully completed in 1961.

When I contemplated the selection of a subject for my thesis, I thought that I had a rare opportunity to think. Therefore, rather than simply selecting a type of building to study, I thought that I should apply myself to addressing the most important subject that I could think of. This got me to recollect my experience as a student of architecture where my professors gave me different and often contradictory comments on my design assignments; something that perplexed me and that I tried to understand since my early days in college. Therefore, I thought that the most important subject I could address would be to explore this issue. Tackling this topic amounted to addressing theory of architecture, and I spent considerable time reading in the university library to find an answer to my query.

I began with writings by famous architects who generally promoted their different styles of design. Then I read books on theory of architecture. Some referred to "good proportions" as prerequisite to good architecture without defining what "good proportions" are. When "good proportions" were defined, they were defined differently by different authors. Generally, I was unable to discern any areas of general agreement in what I read.

However, theory of architecture commonly maintains that architecture involves functional and aesthetic aspects. Starting from this premise, and from the notion that issues relating to functional aspects are amenable to general agreement, I surmised that disagreement and contradiction in the field of architecture probably arise from different preferences relating to the aesthetic aspects of buildings. This position led me to seek answers in the field of aesthetics. So, I read on aesthetics in architecture and aesthetics in general. I also read about experimental aesthetics, and how it failed in its attempts to apply scientific methods in establishing criteria for excellence. Sadly, I ended with a feeling of dissatisfaction similar to the one I got from reading on theory of architecture.

Reading on aesthetics, reference was often made to the subject of perception as key to understanding the experience of aesthetic quality. In my search for clarification of issues, one book led to another, and I read on the physiological and philosophical explanations of perception, and further, on the subjects of psychology, and philosophy in general. Thus, the decision to tackle the subject of theory of architecture as the theme of my Doctoral thesis initiated my drift into philosophy.

My research in philosophy led me to understand how different people disagree in assessing buildings. It can be empirically established that peoples' assessments regarding particular matters could vary from complete agreement by all, which is very rare when large numbers of people are involved, to various degrees of disagreement among different individuals. Two opposing philosophical positions have been developed to interpret this empirical phenomenon.

Some philosophers maintain that assessment is subjective, not objective. The position of this group of philosophers is exemplified in the statement that "beauty is in the eye of the beholder". This means that disagreement in the assessment of a given object results from differences in the eyes, or rather, the minds of different beholders. The differences relate to each beholder's unique make up and life experience. Accordingly, since people and their experiences are not identical, it has been maintained that the assessments of beauty and ugliness, right and wrong, and in certain cases even truth and falsehood, are subjective and thus could vary between different individuals. Furthermore, action of any sort -except some reflexes and logical operations such as mathematics- is based on the value judgment of a beholder, and thus is also subjective and potentially variable. This type of position has been applied by various philosophers in aesthetics, ethics, and theory of knowledge, and holders of this position are referred to as "relativists".

Other philosophers put forth the opposite view of relativism. For example, Plato presented the concept of "universal forms", which classifies aesthetic and moral values together with mathematical relations as entities that exist independently of the beholder, and which humans strive to perceive. I have come to refer to this type of position as "absolutism" to highlight its contrast with relativism. The relativist says that he tends to believe that there are no objective values in the world out there for people to disagree and quibble about. The absolutist on the other hand asserts that "universal forms" exist in the world, and that some astute people are able to perceive them; those who do not should be educated in order to be able to perceive them.

When I started work on my thesis I was a young idealist. I believed in and sought perfection. One of my main motives in selecting the subject of my thesis was that I thought that I could find out what is good and what is bad in the field of architecture. This means, in retrospect, that I held platonic views, and was thus by my own definition an absolutist. From this initial attitude, I dug as deeply as I could in my research to find solid grounds to build on in my platonic endeavor. Alas, I did not find any! Instead, my research led me to switch from absolutism to relativism. My reason for switching is that I did not find any grounds to adhere to absolutism, which usually leads the absolutist to think: "I am right, and all those who disagree with me are wrong"; please note that numerous factions in the USA today feel and act adversely towards each other due to assuming absolutist attitudes in adhering to their differing and often opposing views!

At that time I thought to consistently express my conviction by stating: "I now tend to believe the proposition that value judgment is subjective and potentially variable". And I might add that I never changed my mind about this proposition. Thus: "I do believe that value judgment is subjective and potentially variable".

To sum up, when selecting a topic for my Doctoral thesis, I decided to address the issues that led my college professors to give me conflicting critiques of my projects. Without guidance from my Doctoral supervisor, I drifted into philosophy and became a relativist. My research led me to believe that value judgments are subjective, and that differences in judgment relate to the different unique constitution and experiences of different individuals. This provided the answer to my initial query and explained how my college professors often gave me different critiques of my work: they obtained their graduate degrees from different schools of architecture that embraced different approaches to architectural design!!

This may be a simple common sense conclusion. However, consistent adherence to relativism can lead to serious consequences. It affected my attitudes in thought and in practical matters. Generally, I tend to think of my assessments as my subjective value judgments and preferences, and to present them as such, rather than present them in the form of assertions about the value of an object or an idea. This is reflected in my use of language. Instead of saying "beautiful" or "ugly" I say: "I like", or "I don't like". Also, Instead of saying "good", "bad", and "better", I tend to say "I like", "I dislike", and "I prefer", and instead of saying that an idea is "right" or "wrong", I say: "I agree" or "I disagree" with the idea.

Furthermore, my belief in relativism had a devastating consequence. My supervisor who appreciated my efforts and was prepared to grant me a Doctorate Degree asked me one day: "Can you say anything useful based on your research!?" In the first place, being a relativist, I was not prepared to designate anything I might say as "useful" while thinking that others might consider what I say as "useless" or "bunk"! In addition, I felt that the statement expressing my belief in relativism which resulted from my research is hardly of any use; it simply expresses a personal belief. Accordingly, my response was: "Sorry dear professor, I am unable to say anything that ***could be of use*** based on my research". Thinking this way, led me to abandon my thesis; a sad conclusion to several years of study!!!

Hoping to derive some positive results from many years of research -that I felt might have been spent in vain- I kept trying to find an answer to the question: "Can I possibly say something that could be of use based on my research!?" This question kept haunting me for many years until I found an answer. The answer is expressed in this book!

As the title of the book indicates, I will suggest certain courses for action which, by my own definition, involve numerous subjective value judgments that the reader may or may not agree with. I will try to indicate such instances by saying "I believe" or "I think" such and such. However, common language usage hampers complete philosophical consistency in this respect. For example, the statement: "I believe that there is a problem" still indicates the existence of a problem independently from me; remember Plato, a problem that only astute individuals are capable of perceiving!? To address this conundrum I thought I could highlight such words with single inverted commas, but decided that this would be distractive. Instead, I thought that readers will recognize such words on their own, especially, when they disagree with some of my subjective assessments.

Having expressed my dilemma, I hope that you the reader would not be put off if and when you happen to disagree with some of my statements and continue to read the full text to get the gist of my ideas.

Chapter 2

Systematic Planning as an Effective Tool for Identifying and Solving Problems

After abandoning my thesis I returned to practice architecture around 1965. My belief in relativism did not stifle my action. I chose to continue to live, and needed to earn my living by practicing my profession.

Although initially trained as an architect, I got involved over the years in the related field of urban planning. This led to certain views that are most relevant to the subject matter of this book. Therefore, I will devote this chapter to introducing the field of urban planning, and to express certain results of my experience in the field that pertain to my writing this book.

Urban planning as practiced today is a relatively modern phenomenon. Historically, urban planning efforts usually involved a potentate and an architect, in a way similar to that of an individual commissioning an architect to design a building. The potentate assumed the decision making role as a single client, and the architect tended to address limited physical design parameters in largely intuitive fashion. The general public was rarely involved in the process of urban planning. Potentates in some developing countries and some major developers still approach urban planning in similar fashion, albeit more parameters are now being taken into consideration in the preparation of schemes for urban development than used to be the case in the past.

Contemporary practice commonly involves government authorities and numerous individuals in the decision making process, and attempts to reach agreement regarding action through development of consensuses among numerous entities referred to as the "stake holders". Accordingly, one of the buzz words in the field of urban planning in recent decades is "public participation".

This trend is clearly reflected in certain urban planning efforts, in particular in redevelopment projects that affect the lives of a resident population. Now, it is not uncommon for urban planners to setup shop in the area targeted for such studies and from their location within the community, the planners strive to interact with the local resident, seek their participation in the planning process, and engage the residents in the assessment of conditions and developing consensus for potential action. The reason for this recent trend, I suspect, is that more urban planners are tending to be relativists rather than absolutists who wish to impose their views on others.

The planning process involves numerous steps starting with data collection which is usually undertaken by the entity that commissions a planning study; often a government authority or a private developer. The planner's task is to review available data and information provided by the client, and if needed, gather additional information and often undertake relevant field surveys to complement available data. These activities are undertaken to document existing and past conditions regarding any urban area intended for study. The information gathered generally relates to people and to the physical environment. Information regarding people includes demographic and socioeconomic characteristics. Information regarding the environment covers various facets and conditions of the natural and built environment.

The next step involves analysis of information and

identification of issues. For example, an issue might be the lack of affordable housing to accommodate people working in the inner city. This is followed by consideration of goals and objectives to address the identified issues. A goal usually describes the need for action to address a particular issue; in this case could be: "Provide adequate affordable housing to low income groups in the inner city". An objective relates in turn to the expressed goal, but is further articulated and quantified; in this case could state: "Provide 1000 affordable housing units in the inner city by the year 2030". The significance of involving stakeholders in the planning process can be discerned from this example. Some residents of the inner city may vehemently oppose the construction of affordable housing and kill the project before its inception.

The next step involves analysis of gathered information to identify constraints and opportunities to the realization of expressed goals and objectives. Continuing with the example of affordable housing, an opportunity might relate to the existence of relatively inexpensive vacant land in the inner city that is suitable for accommodating the required number of affordable housing units. A constraint in the same context could relate to the lack of such inexpensive vacant land in the inner city.

This is then followed by the preparation of alternative schemes for urban development. Usually, a number of alternative solutions are conceived. The number of alternatives is often limited to three different options. The potential solutions can vary in nature, and level of detail. Alternative solutions may be conceived at the level of strategies and policies to address the issues and the needs that have been identified, as in the case when alternative strategies are conceived to revitalize the development of a deteriorating inner city. The alternative strategies and associated policies could be conceived in the form of statements that may propose, for example, improving public transportation and reducing property and sales taxes in the targeted area. Alternative solutions may be conceived otherwise in the form of urban development or redevelopment schemes. Also, the alternative schemes may be in the form of urban design projects, for example, to provide housing, roads, infrastructure, community facilities, and pedestrian paths and landscaping in an area of study.

This involves the synthesis and integration of numerous inputs and is usually the responsibility of the planning team's project manager. The alternatives are evaluated through matrices to gauge the extent to which each alternative solution meets each of the goals and objectives that has been previously agreed to; activities that involve evaluation, i.e. subjective value judgment! The alternative scenario or scheme that is considered to most closely meet goals and objectives is selected and proposed for adoption and implementation. The steps involved in implementation, and possible phasing ofdevelopment are usually indicated. Stakeholders would be approached to obtain their approval of proposed action.

A major lesson that I learned from my practice is to consider urban planning assignments in wider special and socioeconomic contexts. For example, when addressing issues in a particular neighborhood I did that in the context of the district, town or city were the neighborhood is located, while covering demographic and socioeconomic parameters. Widening the scope of considerations of different assignment, invariably, revealed issues that I had to address in order to conceive more satisfying solutions. Therefore, generally, I am convinced that lack of consideration of issues within a wider context is likely to compromise my own satisfaction with my urban planning schemes.

Recognition of the above considerations led many clients to demand that areas designated for urban planning studies be considered in wider spatial context. For example, the study of a local area is required to be considered in the context of the district, or the entire town or city in which the local area is located. In similar fashion the study of a new town or city is required to be considered within the context of the region where they are to be located, and the study of a region is usually addressed in the national context. Also, a national urban planning study usually takes into consideration international conditions, since the latter invariably impact considerations at the national level.

Actually, many countries have already commissioned the preparation of comprehensive national development plans; sometimes called master plans, or structure plans, and more recently strategic development plans which describe action for the economic and urban development of their countries.

Generally, the urban planning process is iterative, since conditions constantly change. For example, new roads and highways are often constructed to alleviate traffic congestion. Invariably however, new roads and highways attract progressively more traffic. In turn, vehicular traffic spurs new urban development that increases vehicular traffic and the cycle continues leading to traffic congestion of the newly constructed roads and highways. This usually leads to the reiteration of the planning process.

Urban planning can be classified into two categories: reactive and proactive. The classification into these two types of approach relates to the urban planner's general attitude in addressing issues. The reactive mode could be understood as exemplifying an attitude to cope with issues as they occur. I do not consider this to mean "planning" but rather spontaneous problem solving. Another way of interpreting the term "reactive planning" which I agree with implies the acceptance of particular identified conditions and trends, and assuming that they will prevail in the future. In this sense, the urban planner assumes a reactive attitude towards conditions and trends that he does not wish to change, cannot change, or has no business in changing. The reactive attitude is reflected often in the planner's acceptance of population socioeconomic conditions and trends, as for example, the rate of growth of a particular population.

The proactive mode embodies an attitude to interfere with, and to change conditions and trends. The urban planner assumes a proactive attitude when he thinks that certain conditions or trends need to be changed in order to meet stated goals and objectives. A mixture of both attitudes prevails in practice and applies in all the following types of approaches to urban planning.

Urban planning can be carried out to cope with issues as and when they arise. This is referred to as "crisis planning". As such, I do not consider crisis planning as a form of planning but rather, as a form of reactive problem solving. Sadly, many entities entrusted with planning that I have encountered in my career were more involved   with putting out fires, i.e. spontaneous problem solving.

Finally, urban planning, like architecture, is a field of endeavor that is geared towards action. As such, by my own definition, every step involved in the planning process is driven by individual subjective value judgment. The assessment of existing conditions, the identification of issues, the evaluation and ranking of alternatives and the selection of a preferred alternative are all phrases describing main steps in the planning process. Each phrase includes one or more words that I consider as reflecting the involvement of subjective and potentially variable valuation. I wish to consolidate my views in this respect by citing a few examples.

I gave an outline of urban planning, and indicated the types of activities and the kinds of considerations that are involved in the field. The reader can conceive how the types of activities and the related considerations that I mentioned could be applied to all sorts of activities. When I plan a vacation I may obtain brochures about different areas that I could visit, flip through the brochures, and decide where I will spend my vacation. I would have gone through the steps of data collection, analysis, identification of opportunities and constraints, etc., without necessarily being consciously aware of each of these steps. I may not explicitly express my goals and objectives in having a good time on my vacation, but my mind would have intuitively covered this aspect in a process of evaluation and selection. The difference between urban planning and the planning of everyday activities is that urban planning explicitly expresses the processes that otherwise may be intuitively carried out. This is done in order to reach out to stake holders and seek their feedback and approval.

I would like to point out in this context that no amount of analysis could lead by itself to conceiving a solution. The activities involved in synthesis, in my view, are akin to those involved in an intuitive act of design, and probably involve fuzzy logic. Furthermore, while different parameters may be analyzed by different specialists in an urban planning team, overall synthesis takes place in one mind, often the team leader's mind.

Bottom line, the main outcome of my professional experience in urban planning projects was recognition that the rigorous urban planning process that I used in practice is a powerful tool for problem solving. This recognition is vital to appreciating my proposals for action.

Chapter 3

Application of Systematic Planning to Identify and Address Critical Global Problems

To begin with, let me explain how I generally believe that there is a need for action.

Over the millennia, human conditions have gone through numerous phases of improvements and setbacks. On the whole though, the human predicament has generally improved over time. This is evidenced by the rising age of mortality and the growth of the global population. Accordingly, one could assume that progress would continue without the need for organized interference with prevailing conditions.

However, recent scientific knowledge revealed previously unknown existential threats to survival, and even population growth itself is now damaging the Earth's environment that sustains life.

Also, although research and action to address relevant negative issues is underway, efforts in this vein have not been carried out in an organized and coherent manner. Furthermore, I believe that numerous vital existential issues have not been addressed in a manner commensurate with the extent of their criticality, and therefore, require additional attention.

At some point about thirty years ago, having appreciated the power of systematic planning in problem solving, it occurred to me that it could be possibly applied to identify and address critical global issues!?

As I mentioned in the previous chapter, I am generally convinced of the merits of strategic planning which widens the scope of considerations for planning both in space as well as parameters covered. Years ago, this prompted me to consider the idea of applying systematic planning to identify and address global issues. Furthermore, I thought that if I tried to implement this idea and reached some encouraging results, I might perhaps be able to say something that "could be of use"; i.e., might find an answer to the question that haunted me since the time I abandoned my doctoral dissertation!?

This idea might sound too ambitious and impracticable. Not so however. I have been considering its potential implementation for quite some time and reached the following conclusions.

Two key steps are involved in initiating and carrying out a planning exercise: definition of goals and involving stakeholders in the planning process. Now, mortality statistics indicate that around 1% of the global population commit suicide. Accordingly, one could assume that 99% would accept the goal to: "Preserve human life as long as possible".

Furthermore, if we ask people whether they wish to live in misery for the rest of their lives, they are likely to prefer to live happily ever after. However, happiness is hard to define, and making everybody happy is unlikely. Therefore I thought of the goal in this respect would be at least: "Provide adequate living conditions to all humans".

I have already identified and classified the following threats to human survival and wellbeing: a. Celestial: gamma ray bursts, our sun, and bombardment by meteorites and comets, b. Terrestrial: earthquakes, volcanic eruptions, tsunamis, hurricanes, and tornadoes, c. Biological: aging, and disease, and d. Human related: greed, racism, and aggression.

I have also considered the criticality of the above threats in order to establish priority in addressing them and came to some conclusions in this respect.

For example, a gamma ray burst would obliterate all forms of life on Earth including us. Furthermore, a gamma ray burst would approach us at the speed of light, so we would not be there to realize what hit us! As such, I consider addressing this issue to be a matter of utmost priority.

Also, our sun is predicted to bloat into a red giant engulfing Earth and extinguishing all forms of life on it. However, this is anticipated to occur after five billion years, thus, not constituting a priority for immediate action. On the other hand, the sun's flares can wreak havoc on the Earth's protective magnetic field with potentially serious threats to our survival; perhaps another priority to address.

A large meteorite hitting Earth could lead to our extinction as well as the extinction of many other forms of life on the planet; as had happened twelve billion years ago and led to the extinction of the dinosaurs. Thus, this issue needs to be addressed as a matter of priority.

Earthquakes, volcanic eruptions, tsunamis, hurricanes, and tornadoes, may not lead to extinction. However, they certainly lead to the death and suffering of large numbers of people, and therefore addressing their threats deserves constant attention.

On the other hand, aging and disease have been rigorously addressed and further advances in scientific and medical research are likely to continue to improve the prospects for wellbeing and longevity; according, not necessarily requiring additional attention.

Human action through waging war does need to be addressed as a matter of priority. President Putin's invasion of the Ukraine threatens to escalate to the use of nuclear weapons and potential Armageddon. If not, war still leads to the death and suffering of thousands or millions of people. Also, humans' degradation of the environment is causing more violent weather conditions and is even threatening our existence. Therefore, addressing environmental issues requires immediate and sustained attention.

Last but not least, particular social and political conditions have the greatest impact on human welfare. Dictatorships, democracies, capitalist and socialist orders respectively entail different profound consequences affecting the living conditions of billions of people. According, sociopolitical issues also deserve to be addressed as a matter of priority. Current conditions in the USA illustrate this proposition.

In the USA today, we are experiencing almost dysfunctional political and social conditions. Every now and then we hear that Congress has to act within a few days to avert Government shut down!! The Congress building was attacked by a mob and our elected representatives were forced to flee from the building, and some of them and their families have been physically assaulted; we seem to be on the verge of losing the democratic system that we were once proud of. Furthermore, mass shootings of school children occur on a regular basis claiming the lives of thousands of innocent children. These are but a few examples of the prevailing conditions in the US that cause loss of life and widespread suffering.

Since the US is the most prominent country in the word, what happens here is likely to have global ramifications. Therefore, addressing current sociopolitical conditions in the USA deserves serious consideration.

Having reached the above kinds of conclusions, I realized that I am at the end of my line working alone, and that serious work to address the issues that I have identified would involve the participation of numerous others.

More recently, I thought about how this could be possibly done and contemplated the creation of the Global Planning Center (GPC) to carry the work that I thought was needed; one center that is, not several, because the entity would be charged with the integration of what presently are fragmented efforts.

The scope of work of such a center would be to research, coordinate, and integrate efforts to identify the most critical issues impacting human survival and wellbeing, and promote action to address the identified issues. The disciplines involved are likely to include but not be limited to: cosmology, earth sciences, environmental science, demography, architecture, urban planning, medicine, biology, political science, sociology, psychology, education, and computer science and technology. Numerous entities would be invited to participate in the work, and the GPC would be entrusted with coordination, and integration of the results of research, and proposing courses for action and seeking stake holders' feedback. In short, the center would assume the role of project manager of the numerous diversified and specialized efforts.

The GPC would be intended to function indefinitely. Compared with the Genome Project which sought answers to a particular question and ended once the answers were found, the proposed center's work would be carried out continuously in order to cope with ever changing conditions, while taking advantage of continuing scientific and technological advances.

The GPC could be hosted by a suitable large university or organization that has the resources to pursue the work. Alternatively, depending on the availability of financial resources, an independent entity could be established to carry out the contemplated work. Subsequently, relevant entities would be invited to participate in the center's work, and progress would depend on the availability of manpower resources and funding. All along, the general public would be invited to participate in the GPC's work.

The GPC could be located anywhere in the world. However, I decided to explore the possibility of its creation in the USA. I did that for two reasons: a. due to the US's power and international eminence, whatever happens here is likely to resound in the rest of the world, and thus, have international consequences, and b. should the GPC succeed in its mission in the USA, then credit would be accorded to us Americans for initiating the effort.

The conceptual wide-ranging scope and anticipated continuous duration of such an endeavor scares some that fear that implementation of this idea would cost zillions of dollars. On the other hand however, the nature of the work predicates a phased approach of implementation that could be readily accomplished with modest resources as the first step towards initiation of the GPC work.

For example, sticking with my own expertise, the GPC could explore and comprehensively document the constraints to global urban development from various threats such as earthquakes, tsunamis, volcanoes, hurricanes and tornadoes and rising sea levels, and based on estimates of mortality figures that might result from such events, prepare global graphic representations depicting the extent of danger from these threats. Documenting the dangers of all forms of development in such areas would help in averting disasters such as what happened in Fukushima Daiichi in Japan. Also, research could guide action to avert disasters in existing developed areas; in particular in many coastal cities around the world. Such efforts would save thousands if not millions of lives.

A more demanding task would be to explore the opportunities for suitable urban development and documenting the results of research in the same fashion. This would help in identifying appropriate sites for new towns, cities, and mega-cities to accommodate the growing populations of the world; especially the anticipated billions in China and India.

Recent thinking in this respect indicates that the selection of appropriate sites would depend on the suitability of the topography, for example, flat vs. hilly, and the availability of arable land to grow the food needs of an anticipated population and thus avoid transporting food from remote locations; intensive food production facilities would be built in scattered locations around the city for the same reason.

Yet another worthy avenue of research is to investigate the design of mega-cities in ways that avoid urban sprawl and the extensive use of the automobile to move between different scattered locations as is the case in most existing large cities. This could be achieved through more intensive land use, provision of mass public transportation, encouraging pedestrian movement as well as numerous other methods. Both urban planners and architects could address such an assignment.

The above assignments could be undertaken by university students, and be of use to governmental and private sector entities internationally, and thus, would help in containing the degradation of the natural environment and in addition, could be used to generate funds for the proposed GPC project.

I am convinced of the merits and the feasibility of such efforts, and would be glad to initiate and direct the work of a potential GPC in the USA to prove my point.

Chapter 4

Addressing Human Survival from Natural Threats

I anticipate that gamma ray bursts are likely to be recognized as posing the greatest threat to our survival. This could lead astronomers to consider potential sources of gamma ray bursts, and based on their investigations, space shields would be constructed to divert potential gamma ray bursts form reaching Earth.

As I mentioned earlier, one critical celestial threat is the bloating of the sun that would engulf Earth and extinguish all forms of life on it. However, this is anticipated to occur after five billion years, and accordingly, it is not a high priority issue to address. Therefore, I do not expect any action to be taken in this respect in the foreseeable future; who knows, in five billion years we might have conquered the universe and are able to move stock and barrel to other livable planets. On the other hand though, strong solar flares could conceivably have serious effects on life on Earth. Therefore, I anticipate that systematic planning is likely to lead to the construction of space shields that would divert solar flares from reaching the Earth.

The threats from meteorites and comments bombarding the Earth have been already recognized and ways to address their threat are being investigated by NASA and other space agencies around the world. I foresee that systematic planning would lead to augmenting ongoing current efforts in this respect.

Likewise, the threats to survival from aging and disease are being addressed through scientific and medical research, and therefore, I believe that work in this vein will continue and probably be augmented.

On the other hand, I think that the threats from terrestrial earthquakes, volcanic eruptions, tsunamis, hurricanes, and tornadoes have not been addressed in manner commensurate with the extent of their dangerous consequences. Well, the global urban planning research that I proposed to initiate the work of the GPC would help in this respect by designating areas to avoid and areas to be recommended for urban development internationally. This, in turn, could spur action to remedy existing dangerous conditions.

In the past, international travel and trading of commodities was carried out largely by sea leading to the emergence of numerous port cities. Now, many existing coastal towns and cities around the world are threatened by tsunamis and rising sea levels; for example such as many in Florida. I think that rigorous planning would propose moving the populations of such vulnerable habitats to higher ground, and as a result, I suspect that coastal urban development is likely to recede inland internationally. Alternatively, where it is not practicable to relocate large numbers of people away from vulnerable coastal habitats, dikes and other structures would be constructed to avoid disaster; such as for example those constructed to save Venice from sea flooding.

Also, many existing towns and cities like Napoli for example, lie at the feet of volcanoes. Systematic planning is likely to suggest ways to move the affected populations out of harm's way, or propose ways to save their lives.

Generally, the GPC would prepare a comprehensive list of threats to survival from natural causes based on factual data and information and would propose action to address identified threats. Furthermore, the center would engage affected stakeholders and seek their feedback on proposed courses of action and their funding to ensure implementation.

I will cover the thorny issues relating to the threats to survival from man's action, namely war the degradation of the environment, in the following chapters.

Chapter 5

Constraints and Opportunities to Addressing Problems Relating to Human Action

Let us assume for argument's sake that the GPC is somehow established here in the USA. What could happen then!? In the previous chapter I indicated some possible action relating to addressing survival issues from natural threats including certain practical urban planning activities that could initiate the work of the GPC; I believe that they are relatively straightforward and uncontroversial and suspect that they could be implemented in relatively short order.

I also indicated that addressing all problems relating to human action is likely to be relatively more difficult. To illustrate what I mean by that I will cite historical developments that have led to certain conditions in the USA that I believe would constitute potential serious hurdles to the progress of the GPC's work in the US.

The American form of democracy succeeded in numerous ways. Sadly however, the form of democracy practiced in the USA had major flaws. They can be directly related to the greed demonstrated by the ruling elites including many of those who were presumably "elected by the people" to assume power.

As it is, those who want to be elected to serve in the legislative branches of government -the Congress and Senate- would start by announcing their desire to run for office. Then, in order to have a chance to be elected, a candidate has to spread the word about his/her credentials and views to the general public to convince the voters to vote for him or her. This entails embarking on costly election campaigns and placing advertisements on privately owned newspapers and television stations that exact exorbitant charges. Therefore, candidates for office, if not wealthy themselves, have to ask somebody for money, and the wealthy are often the first to indulge them; usually, only if and when the particular candidate promises to serve their ulterior agendas. Similar conditions apply in the election of the head of the executive branch: the President of the country. Thus, over the decades, the oligarchs exercised their influence over all sorts of politicians and often succeeded in gaining control of both the legislative and executive branches of government. Having achieved that, it became easier to gain control of the judiciary branch embodied in the Supreme Court; since the candidates for the highest court were nominated by the President and approved by the Senate. In this way, the oligarchs often gained overall control of all three branches of Government in the USA and were able to maintain their control of political and social conditions; a notable example of the results of these developments is the recent Supreme Court decision to abolish abortion which robs women from their natural right to control their own bodies!

Also, the political leaders of the USA were aware of the problems of communism, which, in addition to the ruthlessness of communist dictatorial leaders, had to do with stifling the greedy impulses that presumably provide incentive to the creation of wealth to be shared by all. Accordingly, they adopted a capitalist form of economic policy that allowed for incentives to encourage profitable enterprise. This arrangement worked for a while, and indeed succeeded in creating unprecedented wealth in America in the early twentieth century. However, the greed of many entrepreneurs led to a severe economic depression in 1930 which devastated the American people. This led the then President Franklin D. Roosevelt to devise the "New Deal" which introduced a number of laws and programs that provided a measure of financial security to working men and women. FDR's approach succeeded in creating economic growth, while at the same time helping the poor and the middle class whose incomes continued to improve for about fifty years.

However, the prevailing political ideologies in the USA have been generally classified as 'conservative' and 'progressive'. In recent history, conservatives belonged mainly to the Republican Party, and promoted the preservation of 'old values' which mainly benefited the privileged elite and resisted any attempts for change geared to helping the common people. On the other hand, progressives who belonged mainly to the Democratic Party promoted changes that were mainly conceived to help the common people of the middle class and the poor. It is noteworthy in this context that early in twentieth century, progressive leaders organized symposia called "citizen assemblies" that invited large numbers of people of different political inclinations to meet and discuss their divergent views. Invariably, these assemblies resulted in a percentage of conservatives reversing their position, but never the other way around; which can be construed as indicating that progressive views make sense, and that it takes stubborn resistance to reasoning to adhere to conservative views.

The back and forth tide between those who adopted the opposing ideologies of conservatism and progressive idealism was reflected in American political developments. I cannot cover all the examples and details of these developments. I will only cite a notable relatively more recent example that illustrates my case.

Ronald Reagan, a movie star and a staunch conservative was supported by the Republican Party to be elected President of the USA in 1980 and served for two terms. Reagan may not be considered as a greedy leader seeking more power and wealth, perhaps rather, he simply believed in trickledown economics whereby maintaining the status of the wealthy results in creating wealth that eventually passes down to the less privileged citizens. It must be noted though that many of those who supported him were not as benevolent. Irrespective, Reagan proceeded to undo FDR's New Deal. Most notably, he reduced taxation rates on the wealthy, and fired over 11,000 airport traffic controllers who were on strike living an attempt to improve their wages and banned them from civil service for life; thus dealing a record blow to organized labor which strived to improve the wages of working men and women. It is noteworthy that similar developments took place in parallel in England, were the conservative British Prime Minister Margaret Thatcher implemented similar measures; though with less severe consequences in England.

Before I proceed any further, I wish to clarify the meaning of the word "socialism". The online dictionary definition is: "a political and economic theory of social organization which advocates that the means of production, distribution, and exchange should be owned or regulated by the community as a whole." Another definition refers to "democratic socialism" as a political system that aims at fair income distribution and is practiced in Sweden and Denmark. I do not agree with what the first definition proposes and do not suggest its implementation. However, I definitely sympathize with democratic socialism since it attempts to achieve the goal: "Provide adequate living conditions to all humans".

I wish to add that the oligarchs of our capitalist system, for their own ulterior motives, made every effort to indoctrinate the American people to fear the mention of "socialism" by citing the worst aspects of its implementation; many Americans actually panic when the word "socialism" is uttered!

Back to historical developments.

President Reagan, like other former US presidents such as John F Kennedy, felt that socialism, which was being practiced with relative success in the USSR whose influence was spreading internationally, presents a threat to American Democracy and Capitalism. It must be admitted that the practice of socialism in the Union of Soviet Socialist Republics, the USSR, including Russia and its satellite states had serious flaws. Among those, the suppression of free speech and the abuse and even assassination of anyone who dared to oppose the ruling regimes. Therefore, Reagan had a reasonable argument to oppose the USSR. At any rate, Reagan kept increasing US military spending and was able to drain the resources of the USSR who was trying to keep pace with the US's military might. Ultimately this led to the collapse of the USSR in 1991. Thus Reagan defeated the idea of socialism at its source.

I never regretted the demise of the USSR. However, I believe that Reagan's main motive in bringing Russia to its knees was to buttress the status of Capitalism both in the USA and abroad, and to quench the attempts to consider socialist ideas that were emerging here in the USA at the time.

Subsequently, the US oligarchy of individuals and corporations continued to join hands to further their agenda. Their concerted efforts over a few decades succeeded in attaining ever more of their egocentric goals. They influenced government action in many ways in order to further enrich themselves, their families and those who controlled power, as the rest of the people became poorer, thus creating an astounding wealth gap between the rich and poor in America. Statistics of conditions in the USA in the early twenty first century show that the wealthiest top 2% of the population owned more of the country's wealth than the less privileged 98%. Also, the heads of many corporations were often paid more than a 1,000 times the average wage of their employees.

A glaring example of the plight of working men and women relates to employment statistics. To my mind, full employment is something to strive for; all would be able to make a living. But no! Here in the USA when unemployment statistics approach 5% the crap hits the fan. The reason given for that is fear of inflation. The argument given is: If all are employed, more money would be available for spending on buying goods and services, which in turn would lead to rising prices and inflation! Bull!! In the first place we need to ask: Who raises the price of goods and services, is it really the 'concept' of supply and demand!? Rather, I am convinced that shunning full employment relates more to employers' fear that labor shortages can lead to demands for more equitable compensation by the working people.

Furthermore, and perhaps more seriously, the quest of the oligarchs led over time to the election of ever more corrupt politicians, and the success of such candidates in elections often implied lying about their credentials and views, and ultimately to the emergence of a society that was unable to differentiate between truth and falsehood. The election of past President Trump is a glaring example of this predicament. Actually, in their quest to attain political power, Trump and his allies and supporters have competed for conceiving ever more glaring lies, misinformation, and conspiracy theories; sadly, since the more outrageous disinformation tended to bring about more success at the polling stations!?

Now, the practice of democracy depends on apprising the electorate of factual information that allows them to make informed decisions about issues, and thereby help the voters to elect candidates for office who would address their needs. Instead, the emerging paradigm which obscures falsehood from reality is leading to the erosion of the foundations of the practice of democracy itself.

This sad development cannot be attributed only to the conniving action of the capitalist oligarchs. Numerous US citizens could be construed to share the blame. A large block of the voting public in the USA estimated at over 30 percent of the electorate believed the lies and the misleading rhetoric of many oligarchs who strived for more wealth and power, and tended to elect the kind of politicians who had no sincere intentions to address their legitimate plight. Unfortunately, the common citizens who elected such politicians fell for the oligarchs propaganda and misinformation and thought of social reforms that were conceived to their own advantage as reflecting a 'welfare state' that would only benefit undeserving lazy 'others', who sit around doing nothing except drawing on social benefits and thereby enjoying the fruits of other people's labor. Current developments in the USA clearly demonstrate this sad condition.

Now, if the GPC is established in the USA and proposed to address the degradation of the environment as a vital issue, vehement followers of past President Trump are likely to disagree with considering environmental conditions as a vital issue worthy of addressing as matter of priority. They may not only disagree with considering the topic of the environment as a matter of priority, but moreover, they might even organize to block its consideration by the GPC!

Nowadays, the conservative camp is not amenable to reasoning; such as for example considering the facts and the evidence supporting a certain proposition; one of the main tenets of the proper practice democracy. The potential GPC has to contend with this reality, and the question arises as to how to cope with this predicament.

A buzz word among progressives in this context is that "conservatives are not going to go away". However, go away they shall; they are mortal like the rest of us! I wish to add in this context that the recent discipline of conflict resolution reminds us that both parties to a conflict typically think they're right and the other side is wrong; remember absolutism!! It suggests avoiding escalating tensions with threats and provocative moves, and to calmly seek reconciliation with whomever we happen to disagree with. Therefore, although I do not appreciate the attitudes of many conservatives, I do wish them longevity and understand that their beliefs and actions relate to their unique personal experiences. Obviously, I wish that some would consider factual information and change their political posture. Moreover, I hope that their children and grandchildren would be brought up to be more reasonable!!? An eventuality that could perhaps materialize in a generation or two!?

Well, "generation" is defined as a thirty year span of time. That is how I suggest that the resolution of global issues could take as many as sixty years.

On the other hand, I believe that certain encouraging developments could be helpful in achieving the expressed GPC goals. The action of certain groups in society could be instrumental in achieving this end. Most notably, educators who are usually more enlightened members of their communities have made and continue to make concerted efforts to address aggressive impulses and the fear and resentment of others. Young children of different color and ethnicity are being encouraged to play together. These efforts are helping in overcoming the sentiments of racism and the resentment of others and are encouraging collaboration and fraternity. Ultimately, over several decades, the concerted efforts of educators could lead to ever growing numbers of younger generations who dismiss the racist and hateful rhetoric of ill meaning politicians and to belief in peaceful co-existence and human cooperation.

Furthermore, educators could also highlight the fact that the real threats to human survival are not other humans, but rather that the threats to our survival and wellbeing are primarily aging and disease, the degradation of the earth's environment, catastrophic events relating to earth's dynamism such as volcanic eruptions, earthquakes and tsunamis, as well as sundry cosmological threats from comets, meteorites and gamma ray bursts. Educators could stress that these are the real threats that we need to mobilize ourselves and our resources to cope with, rather than waste lives and resources fighting with each other.

It could take decades for the educator's efforts to bear fruit, and generations to address the obstinacy of numerous fanatical religious groups around the world who tend to hate all others; especially some entrenched groups in USA and in the Middle East. However, education could instill the positive attitudes of working together to secure the existence and general wellbeing of all based on the concept of the common good. Over time, this could pave the way for the emergence of a self-sustaining system where people participate in the creation of their collective resources and sharing them equally.

I must add in this context that certain conservative entities in the USA are working vehemently to block the efforts of progressive educators by banning and removing books that address racism from school libraries; reminiscent of "Chrystal Nacht" in Germany, when the Nazis burned piles of books that they did not approve of in preparation for the Jewish Holocaust and the massacre of millions of innocent people.

Also, although some world leaders in the past were females, such as the proverbial Queen of Sheba and Queen Cleopatra, and the more recent queens of England and Scotland, the great majority of historical monarchs and emperors, as well as those in top power positions were men. Many of the male leaders were greedy for evermore power and wealth to the point of leading their people to war to fulfill their insatiable greed. Such male leaders of olden countries and empires must be held responsible for waging wars and creating many dire conditions for their subjects and others; the more recent World Wars One and Two are but recent examples of the death and destruction that men in power are capable of bringing about.

Encouraging relevant developments relate to the circumstances of women in society which are likely to have significant positive impacts on people's lives as well as on international affairs. Women constantly strived for equality with men, and eventually did achieve that in democratic societies and earned the right to vote. This allowed them to affect developments through exercise of their voting power.

Also, in the twentieth century women began to be increasingly more involved in politics and to seek leadership positions in government. Thankfully, many did succeed, and by the late twentieth and early twenty first centuries they were almost on par with male politicians. On the whole, female altruistic instincts tend to dampen racist attitudes, as well as the aggression of male leaders and politicians. There is reason to believe that this trend will continue to the advantage of all.

Containing nationalistic fervor could take decades to attain. However, historically in the early twentieth century many world leaders began to realize the futility of wars and the enormous destruction and loss of life that they entail, and the international community agreed to form The League of Nations to act as a forum to resolve conflicts among nations. The League of Nations was rendered defunct and was replaced later with The United Nations, which although not effective in preventing international conflicts and strife, did perform a positive role in international affairs which lasted for many decades. Further developments in this vein are likely to continue.

Also, European leaders who suffered from the horrific results of world Wars One and Two realized the dangers of nationalism. War is defined as armed conflict between sovereign nations. If none exist, there would be no more wars. Realizing this fact, political leaders in Europe managed to form the European Union; the EU. Sadly however, recent developments threaten the existence of the EU; one more reason for me to write this book. I hope that developments both at the national and international levels over several decades could succeed in dampening nationalistic fervor and prevent international conflicts.

I wish to add that applying the rational systematic approach that I propose is likely to expedite progress on addressing and resolving global issues and thus, it might take less than sixty years to accomplish the task.

Chapter 6

Addressing Problems Regarding Human Wellbeing

I fear that action to improve the quality of life of the common people is likely to take a long time to attain. I expressed my concerns in this respect which mainly relate to the lack of proper practice of democracy in the USA at present, and indicated that overcoming this hurdle might take two generations to surmount.

Next, I will consider additional conditions in the USA that illustrate this proposition, namely, by considering what we started from as a nation in respect of human wellbeing and how it could possibly evolve.

The Declaration of Independence of the USA from the British Empire which ushered the initiation of our existence as an independent country and inspired the formulation of our Constitution states:

"We hold these truths to be self-evident, that all men are created equal, that they are endowed by their Creator with certain unalienable Rights, that among these are Life, Liberty and the pursuit of Happiness."

The Declaration reflects serious deficiencies. For example, it refers to "all men", without any mention of women! Also, it mentions endowment by a "Creator" thus invoking religious beliefs that many agnostics and atheists do not subscribe to. In addition, the founding fathers who conceived the Declaration owned slaves who could not experience "Liberty" and had scantly any chance for "the pursuit of Happiness". Furthermore, "Happiness" is hard to define; especially for "all". Therefore the statement regarding "the pursuit of Happiness" is of no consequence.

It should be noted also that the equality of all did not apply in the early stages of the American experiment. For example, the slavery of African Americans continued until abolished in 1865, after which they earned the right to vote only in 1870. Also, women did not have the right to vote until 1920.

By contrast, I imagine that should the GPC be established, it would define the goal relating to human wellbeing to state:

"All humans are equal, and are entitled to adequate shelter, sustenance, health care and education,"

Please note that reference to "all humans" would include men, women, and gay and transgender individuals, and that gay and transgender result from genetic and early life experience.

The associated objective of the GPC would define "adequate", suggest dates for implementation of proposed action and its costs, and poll the people to seek their feedback and support.

Another vital potential development that could help in augmenting and securing the wellbeing of US citizens would address political issues.

In the USA today, we have Democrats who -perhaps half heartedly- are trying to help the common people, and Republicans who are vehemently working to promote the cause of the wealthy. However, I can imagine the following developments that might unfold over some decades and lead to the improvement of the predicament of common US citizens.

From a personal perspective I have appreciated our democratic political order. However, as I mentioned earlier, I am convinced that recent political developments are threatening the continuation of democratic rule in the USA. The practice of democracy depends on apprising the electorate of factual information that allows them to make informed decisions. Well, conditions in this respect had deteriorated to a historical low during the Trump Presidency in the USA. I suspect though that things could get better later, in the first place, by restoring functional democratic rule.

In the short term, a third party might emerge in the US that could resolve the dichotomies of the two party system. Later on, and more importantly, the old guard of politicians mainly relied on financial campaign contributions from wealthy individuals and corporations to get elected and attain their privileged positions. Therefore, they clung to power to continue to enjoy their privileges and to return the favors of their mentors. As such the old guard had a vested interest in maintaining these arrangements, since changing the status quo would amount to shooting themselves in the foot. Progressively however, US elections could potentially bring a fresh breed of younger better educated benevolent men and women to power.

By contrast to existing conditions, a new breed of leaders would not have the same interests of the old guard, and many among them would believe in the merits of direct democratic rule compared with representative democracy and would act to spread the use of direct voting by the public in addressing important issues through referenda for example. Advances in telecommunication technologies would render the direct involvement of the electorate more practicable and would help in spreading the application of direct democracy in the USA. The new system could be called Electronic Direct Democracy, EDD, and would be enshrined in a new Constitution. Electronic devices similar to present smart phones could be given to all voting adults who would be polled about all sorts of relevant issues and their votes and comments would be tabulated by computers and used to reach decisions for action; this function could be implemented also through smart TVs in people's homes. Since the majority of people are likely to approve measures to improve the quality of their own lives, one could expect action towards this end to eventually take place.

Adopting EDD would resolve one of representative democracy's major weaknesses as it is practiced today, namely, by all together eliminating the need for politicians and thus avoiding the problems they tended to create.

Furthermore, I imagine that a new Constitution would define "Government" as groups of the citizens selected by computers to serve two-year terms in a hierarchy of administrative offices at the neighborhood, district, city, region, and national levels. Computers would prepare short lists of three individuals qualified to serve at all levels of government, and rank the candidates based on their respective qualifications and personal disposition. The top candidate would be first approached to secure his or her acceptance of the nomination. If agreeable, the public is approached to endorse the candidate. If not, the next qualified candidate would be approached, and the process would be repeated until a qualified and willing candidate is identified and proposed for endorsement and approval by the people.

The functions of government official would mainly amount to managing and providing guiding human input to the arrays of computers that process relevant information at the various levels of government. Computers would keep records of the demand and supply of all goods and services as well as potential changes as necessary to meet the people's expressed needs and wishes. Officials at the various levels of government would communicate to coordinate the adequate provision of goods and services to meet changing needs by modifying the allocation of both material and human resources to meet demand. As such, the function of the government would be to facilitate the implementation of desired action by the people; truly reflecting the adage "Government for the people by the people".

Another possible meaningful development could be replacing the Dollar with electronic Purchasing Units, PUs, and agreed to mandatory social benefits and minimum rates of compensation of all workers would be directly deposited into peoples' accounts in a manner similar to present day social security benefits. The PUs would be available on income cards -not credit cards- and be available for people to cover their living expenses. Thus, people's basic needs for survival and a decent existence would be fully met and guaranteed by the government. This in turn could have significant consequences.

To begin with it would eliminate the class of greedy individuals and corporations who used to usurp the fruits of the efforts of the working classes to enrich themselves. For example, there would be no banks and financiers to lend money and charge exorbitant interest rates on their loans to the people who needed housing or expensive medical services, and no entities that provide healthcare and medication for profit. Also, these conditions would cure many societal ills and entail major improvements compared with current conditions. For example, there would be no reasons to commit crime and theft, therefore, there would be no need for a police force, courts, judges, lawyers or prisons; compared with current conditions in the USA where running prisons is privatized for profit, leading to the corruption of the judicial system that often rules to incarcerate hundreds of thousands of people for minor offenses to enrich those who run the prisons.

Also, those in charge of implementing the new order would have learned from historical precedents that switching to a new order, and in particular abolishing certain aspects of capitalism is not an easy task to accomplish. For example, the mistake of abolishing ownership rights which was tried and failed in earlier experiments in applying socialism would not be repeated. Therefore, I believe that the right of ownership of property and certain enterprises would be maintained but regulated to avoid negative impacts on the general public. Generally, the new guard of leaders, in coordination with the general public, would ensure that major transitions are pursued gradually, and attempt to minimize the infliction of painful conditions on anyone, including the wealthy.

Conditions in the former United Kingdom in the twentieth and twenty first centuries would provide an example of how this could be achieved. The Lords and Ladies of the British aristocracy, whose stature and wealth were usually endowed by the ruling monarchs in recognition of their services to the Crown, lived in lavish mansions and castles with dozens of servants and employees. In addition, male aristocrats were appointed to the House of Lords where they served to further the causes of their Monarchs, and were accorded substantial privileges for their services. However, increasing taxation rates gradually reduced the wealth of the aristocracy. Eventually, in order to maintain their standard of living, many opened their residences to the general public to visit for a fee. Ultimately, their residences effectively functioned as museums, and in some cases they lived in them as custodians. Such gradual approaches are likely to be adopted during the transition towards a new societal order in the USA.

Last but not least, education would teach people to respect and treat each other with humility; thereby eliminating major conflicts. The only remaining conflicts would occur at the personal level, perhaps reflected in minor spats, and would be addressed by specialized counselors at no charge. Instead of greedy entrepreneurs, the only people accorded special status and more generous compensation would be those who volunteer to work in certain dangerous occupations that are needed to secure human survival and wellbeing.

Ultimately, the new order would be established to the advantage of the needy and the poor, without inflicting undue pain on the wealthy.

Chapter 7

Potential Global Developments

In the previous Chapter 1 cited certain potential positive developments in the USA. If achieved, they could spur similar global developments and spread internationally.

In the past, the USA had taken steps to achieve positive relations with different countries mainly by encouraging international trade. Sadly, large American business corporations took advantage of trade agreements to use cheap labor in developing countries to maximize their profits, which led to the loss of thousands of jobs in the USA. This led the disaffected labor forces in the USA to abhor the prospect of globalization; a fact that past President Trump capitalized on in his quest to attain political power.

However, I believe that the efforts of educators and the increasing involvement of women in politics in the future would not only dampen racist attitudes between people of different color and ethnicity, but also between peoples of different nationality. Such a development could encourage the spread of the idea of globalism which was quite popular among many progressive thinkers in the late twentieth and early twenty first centuries. The ebbing of nationalistic fervor and the attitudes of new progressive leaders could lead to action towards this end.

Therefore, I suspect that a new breed of leaders in the USA would have no gripe about globalization; on the contrary, they are likely to appreciate its potential merits which have been already demonstrated in the European experiment of the European Union; the EU. Accordingly, it is likely that they would initiate action towards forming unions with neighboring countries; who I suspect by then would have appreciated the merits of the political and economic developments in the USA. If so, the new political guard in the US is likely to move to unify the USA, Canada, and Mexico to form a United States of North America, the USNA.

The USA would formally request the two neighboring countries to consider the proposition. The US's request is likely to be endorsed by large majorities in both countries, and all three nations subsequently would agree to participate in investigating potential future unification. An agreement to this effect could follow, and the three nations would agree to adopt one major principle, namely, to use direct democratic methods to guide their action in order to engage all their citizens in the processes of unification and the conception of a new form of governance.

The first step towards the implementation of this approach would be to set up adequate communication channels with the people through interactive devices such as smart phones and TVs, and the three nations would engage in the implementation of the idea of unification via Electronic Direct Democracy. It should be noted that although the application of direct democracy was practiced in ancient Greece, it was never practicable to pursue it on such a large scale if it were not for the great advances in telecommunication technologies that had been achieved in preceding decades.

The next step would involve the preparation of a formal referendum seeking acceptance of unification under one government which is likely to be accepted and designated as the USNA. This could be followed by formidable preparations to conceive the structure and details of a new order of governance. Thousands of delegates including heads of former governments, scientists across the full spectrum of research and application, together with experts in diverse fields of expertise and interests would be drafted to participate in the processes of conceiving the new order while seeking feedback from the populations of the three countries.

It could take a decade from the initial acceptance of the idea of unification to the actual establishment of a functioning unified government. However, such a development would have global ramifications. It would echo in Europe, and continue to echo back and forth reinforcing the progressive cause with significant international consequences. Most notably, moves to dissolve the EU would be eventually reversed by a majority of EU citizens in democratic fashion, and the EU could grow to include more countries to the East, such as former Russia; even the Swiss, who are fiercely nationalistic, are likely to finally agree to join the EU.

The success of the socio-political systems initiated in the USA and the USNA would be eventually appreciated globally, and the trend towards their global adoption would grow over time. Accordingly, it would not be farfetched to anticipate the formation of a Global Government following the USNA's EDD example sometime in the future.

Eventually, the UN member nations would consider global unification and the formation of a Global Government using the UN premises in New York City as its official seat. This would entail abolishing all former independent nations, and totally eliminating competition and potential aggression between independent countries, and thus the need for arming for defense against aggression.

This in turn will free substantial resources for use towards constructive rather than destructive ends. In addition, the troves of guns, rifles, cannons, tanks, missiles and atomic warheads would all be dismantled and recycled for use in construction projects and in the manufacture of consumer goods. This way humanity would eventually succeed in addressing the main historic problems that negatively affected our existence and wellbeing throughout history.

I can't help but make a final comment. As I mentioned earlier, during his tenure the former US President Trump reversed local and international action to protect the environment, reneged on international accords, openly admired the dictatorial leaders of his time, incited divisions among Americans, and denigrated the idea of socialism. In his address to the General Assembly of the UN in 2019 he vowed that the USA will never be a socialist country, and that those who promote globalization are losers. He declared that the motive behind his actions was, in his words: "To make America great again". It is uncanny that the adoption of diametrically opposing views and strategies by his successors could lead the USA to regain the moral authority that it had enjoyed at various intervals in history and to its acceptance as the leading initiator of a new glorious global order.

With all of these achievements, will we then be able to live happily ever after? Not necessarily. I will explain next.

Chapter 8

Stubborn Issues that May Defy Resolution

Back to living happily ever after!

With very few exceptions, most of us prefer to hang on to life for as long as possible. Furthermore, during our life spans we strive to pursue happiness and to avoid all sorts of negative feelings. Sadly however, our human predicament does not allow for complete fulfillment of such aspirations. I will explain some of the underlying reasons for this predicament. I will start by addressing issues relating to human mortality.

Our evolution on Earth led us to being mortal creatures that are also susceptible to a myriad of diseases and mutating viral infections. In spite of all the significant scientific and medical advances that have led to combating many sorts of disease and to prolonging our lives, our achievements have not succeeded in preventing our mortality due to aging, or our death from sundry life threatening conditions.

Many causes of death relate to the dynamic geological nature of Mother Earth which is reflected in major weather storms, hurricanes, tornadoes, earthquakes, volcanic eruptions, and tsunamis. While we might succeed in making progress in addressing and mitigating these threats to our lives, they are likely to continue to claim the lives of many people for some time in the future.

Also, cosmic related threats to our existence such as the potential bombardment by comets and meteorites pose grave risks to our survival. Although we might take numerous steps to cope with this particular kind of threats, the measures we might take may not be fool proof. On the other hand the threat to survival from a gamma ray burst is probably impossible to predict or prevent; they approach us at the speed of light, and if one happens to target Earth we would all perish without being aware of what hit us; on the other hand, our sun's anticipated bloating to a red giant that would eventually engulf the Earth is anticipated to start in about five billion years; so we have some time to think about this one.

Accidents are yet another source of concern. They can cause minor injuries, serious maiming injuries, as well as death. Although we could make considerable progress in reducing their incidence, they are likely to happen no matter what we do.

Irrespective of the causes of mortality, history confirms the extent to which people were concerned about death. For example, the ancient Egyptians mummified the corps of their kings and queens and built colossal tombs to preserve their bodies in the hope of resurrection in the future; the great Pyramids of Giza are the most notable case in point.

The evidence for people's concerns about mortality is clearly discernible in monotheist religions, which implicitly recognize the issue that prevailed for thousands of years. They also offer ways to address it.

Judaism, for example, offered a scenario whereby life never ends, and that upon apparent death on Earth, the soul continues to live and rises to Heaven. Islam and Christianity offered a more definitive scenario indicating that God, who created the Universe in ten days, has preordained a date in the future when all people will be reincarnated and judged for their deeds on Earth. Based on the assessment which will be carried out by God's designated Angels, if a person sinned, he or she would be sent to the inferno of Hell to burn, in some cases for forever. Alternatively, if he or she was virtuous, he or she would go to Heaven and enjoy a delightful existence forever.

These scenarios certainly had a positive impact on human ethical behavior for millennia. In addition, they alleviated the fear arising from facing certain death. Actually, the promise of the persistence of 'the soul' and the promise of an afterlife were major incentives that drove billions of people to believe in monotheist religions over the centuries. Sadly however, there is no scientific evidence supporting the promise of an afterlife as described in various religions.

Bottom line: at least here on Earth, each of us will eventually die. Some of us believe in an afterlife in heaven which helps them cope with this depressing predicament. Others such as agnostics and atheist are not in a position to avail themselves of comforting ideas in this respect, and therefore are forced to accept the reality of death. At any rate however, the death of loved ones evokes feelings of sadness which we will inevitably continue to experience. I have personally experienced this upon the death of my grandparents, my father and mother, uncles and aunts, my dear wife, and many of my dearest friends. Accordingly, the fact of mortality is also associated with generating negative feelings in the minds of those who continue to live. So, at least for these reasons we might as well forget living happily ever after.

In addition, the negative feelings associated with the loss of members of family and friends are not the only ones that stifle our hopes for eternal bliss. There are numerous other causes of suffering and discontent. Although not necessarily menacing, they do evoke unpleasant feelings and therefore are still worthy of consideration and debate.

For example, our living conditions unfold in various unique different ways that shape our individual personalities. Thus, we are not identical in our makeup; even twins and siblings develop different personalities. However, we live together and need to continually interact with each other. Inevitably, this fact leads to many conflicts due to our respective varied beliefs, ideas, and interests that in turn lead to negative feelings.

The most notable and wide spread example of this fact relates to a particular type of relationships. Namely, the relations between men and women; oh, to avoid potential recrimination I considered saying the relations between women and men, but decided to stick with the more common traditional usage. To begin with, the fact that certain problems between men and women have persisted over the centuries, is clearly and concisely expressed in the adage: "You can't live with them, and you can't live without them".

No doubt that men and women differ in many serious ways. In addition to the obvious differences in biological constitution and appearance, they also differ in psychological makeup. So what!? The French say: "Vive la difference", meaning, long live the differences between men and women. Ok, so be it, perhaps the differences add salt and pepper to male/female relations without which we might be led to a bland and tasteless existence. Irrespective however, let us consider some of the differences and their consequences.

Some of the main issues between men and women relate to their different attitudes towards sex. Females conceive offspring, foster babies in their womb, and are incapacitated during nine months of gestation followed by a long period of breast feeding and generally caring for their offspring. These conditions resulted in women being relatively more apprehensive of the consequences of having sex, compared with men who generally and basically just desired more of it due to their strong instinctive urge to spread their genes.

Another important condition affecting the difference in sexual drive between males and females relates to their respective physiological constitutions. Women stop ovulating and bearing children, which is their main 'raison d'être', at about age 50. They experience the strong emotions associated with menopause, and as they get older, start gradually to lose interest in sex. On the other hand, the drive for sex in men, although waning over the years, remains relatively strong for much longer. This fact of life led to serious problems between men and women in the past, and in spite of concerted efforts to address them, issues continue to prevail in this respect; at least from a male perspective.

Generally, I suspect that males were, and will continue to be more demanding for sex, while females were and will continue to be less demanding. This, in turn led men to be generally more promiscuous compared with women. With very few exceptions to the rule, such conditions prevailed over the millennia and continue to prevail today. They lie at the root of many serious issues between men and women.

Another source of problems relates to the fact that the brains of men and women have important structural differences which affect the release of hormones, thus affecting emotional states and behavior; a notable example in women is the onset of menopause with its known symptoms, and the tendency to be more moody compared with men. On the other hand the release of testosterone in men aggravates the issues relating to their sexual drive. These differences continue to be reflected in everyday relations between the sexes and are responsible for numerous types of arguments conflicts, and spats.

At any rate, the fact that monotheist religions addressed the issues between men and women confirms both their existence and persistence over the millennia. Monotheist religions though often provided differing solutions to the inherent problems, thus confirming the elusive nature the inherent thorny issues.

On the one hand, all monotheist religions promoted fidelity in marriage. On the other however, both Judaism and Islam ordained that adulterous women be stoned to death, with no comparable punishment for the undoubtedly more numerous adulterous men. Islam, recognizing men's relatively stronger urge for sex compared with women, allowed -though not encouraged- men to marry up to four wives, and furthermore, to acquire as many concubines as they could afford; as demonstrated in a sultan's harem. Catholicism, recognizing the tendency for promiscuous behavior by both men and women, ordained infidelity as a cardinal sin and prescribed an altogether different solution: a man and a woman are to remain married for life, 'until death do us part'. In addition, Catholicism ordained celibacy for their priests and nuns in an effort to eliminate sexual issues from interfering with the lives of their clergy; a move that backfired with well documented and deeply disturbing consequences.

Thankfully, scientific investigation of the issues that affect the two genders has succeeded to a great extent in containing inherent problems through hormonal treatments and other methods that aim to mitigate the effects of the physiological and psychological differences between men and women. Sadly though, many issues still linger unresolved. However, in the future couples may have recourse to expert conflict resolution counselors who would provide help in addressing their particular problems. The implementation of such measures, spats would rarely come to blows as used to be often the case in the past; especially by men who abused their spouses physically, psychologically, and emotionally, and of course vice versa perhaps to a lesser extent in the case of women abusing their spouses.

Time for a conclusion: no happiness ever after, at least for the foreseeable future. Generally, the obstacles to attaining our aspirations to live happily forever relate to a variety of factors all of which are inherent in nature, i.e. to conditions that are largely outside of our control at least for some time. Some of the natural causes relate to our own evolution and environment on Earth, while others relate to cosmic conditions. Accordingly, since our human predicament exacts an unavoidable price on our existence, all we can do is to try to contain conflicts with each other, and to control our feelings of grief and sorrow and not let them overwhelm our daily lives. This way, we might be able to make the best of our lives while we continue to live.

Ultimately, perhaps there is still hope for fulfilling our aspirations. Anthropology tells us that the earliest homo-sapiens evolved perhaps less than 300,000 years ago. Judging by what we have been able to accomplish during this time span, and the accelerating pace of scientific and technological advances that we continue to achieve, perhaps we might be able to succeed against all odds in our efforts to live happily forever sometime in the not too far future. In the mean time, we must try to avoid creating problems for ourselves, and in particular, abstain from any action that might degrade the environment that sustains our existence.

Conclusion

Well, I spoke my peace! I proposed to address global issues by applying a rational proven method of problem solving and explained how my ideas in this respect have evolved over several decades. In addition, I expressed how the implementation of my proposals for action could possibly unfold, and what conditions might result from the implementation of my proposals. You the reader may or may not like my suggestions for action or the potential results of their implementation. Whichever way, it is now up to you to participate in shaping our collective future by voting and by expressing your views. I must add that the establishment of the GPC would provide a unique ideal forum for all to do just that.

Furthermore, I contemplated how we Americans could lead the efforts to identify and address global problems. However, I wish to stress that we would not be in a position to do this until we put our own act together, mainly, by restoring the practice of democracy in our own country, and by changing some of our laws, such as for example, laws regarding gun ownership and abortion.

It should be noted also that if we miss the opportunities to act rationally in matters relating to human survival and wellbeing, we could conceivably continue to drift towards an unknown future involving the suffering and death of millions of people, and perhaps even the extinction of the human race.

Above all, please keep in mind that I hold no grudge against any individual or group of people, and suggest that you the reader would assume a similar attitude. Let us all try to forget our differences, control the negative impulses of hate and aggression, and instead, trust our common positive human instincts of love and compassion.

On the personal level, I have finally found the answer to the question that haunted me since I aborted my doctorate dissertation: Hurrah, I have now conceived some ideas that "could be of use"!!! Furthermore, I am proud to say that what I conceived does not merely suggest how to make a good omelet; it addresses issues of more potential significance.